YOU HAVE BEEN WARNED!

A COMPLETE GUIDE TO THE ROAD

FOUGASSE & McCULLOUGH

THE BRITISH LIBRARY

First published in 1935 by Methuen & Co.

This edition published in 2013 by
The British Library
96 Euston Road
London NW1 2DB

British Library Cataloguing in Publication Data
A catalogue record for this publication is available from
The British Library

ISBN 978 0 7123 5899 6

Printed in China

INTRODUCTION

ACCORDING to statistics, there is in Great Britain one car to every 33 persons—that is to say, one to drive it, two to give advice from the back seat, one to oil and grease thoroughly and remove all tools, three to step in front of it and one to visit them and eat their grapes, one to devise means for speeding it up and four to devise means for slowing it down, one to draw pictures in the dust on the back, one to keep on taking it in part exchange, two to salute at cross-roads, fifteen to lean their bicycles against it at traffic stops, and one to fail to understand what's come over everybody nowadays.

It is to the last of these that this book is addressed.

CODE IN THE HEAD

" O, to be in England, now that April 's there."

THE intending road-user, to get the fullest enjoyment from his pursuit (as it usually becomes), should begin with the study of the Highway Code. This is the Road-User's Statute of Liberty and Magna Carta of the Road, price one penny. It is also the little blue book that used to lie on the hall table.

It begins with the warning that "*A failure on the part of any person to observe any provision of the highway code shall not render that person liable to criminal proceedings but any such failure may be relied upon to make it so hot for him he won't know the difference.*"

There follows a Foreword by the Minister of Transport, beginning: "*When in the course of human*

" You'd hardly know we were moving."

3

On pleasure bent.

events——" and ending "*——life, liberty, and the pursuit of happiness*"—or words to that effect.

We then have The Code itself.

To Drivers of Motor Vehicles
(especially Motor Cyclists)

1. Never do anything unless you can see that it is safe to do so.

To Cyclists

2. Never do anything unless you can see . . .

To Pedestrians and Drivers of Horse-Drawn Vehicles
(and also to the horse)

3. Never do anything.

Finally there is an illustrated Appendix entitled "*Signals that every Road-User should know.*" This portrays the progress of a weak and not very estimable character who is for ever changing his mind

4

as to where he wants to go.   His contempt for the
law in driving a car without the statutory mirror
shows that he will be up to no good if he gets there.
This, however, is doubtful in view of the fact that
he has neither windscreen wiper nor spare wheel, and
that his car is quite evidently on its last legs.

" Sorry, but I'm a stranger here."

SECTION II

SIGNS AND WONDERS

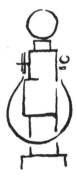

" The haunt of the seamew."

**Famous
Last Words**

" Which is the
throttle ? "

SIGNS AND WONDERS

BEFORE embarking on the road, the novice should of course be familiar with the signals likely to be made by other drivers.

So far as we know there is no book that gives anything like a complete list. The Highway Code, good as it is in every other way, only prints nine examples, eight of which are merely such as would be given by an experienced driver under ordinary circumstances. Thus they represent only a small proportion of the signals actually used, and, to the driver who wishes to know the meaning of the signals sent out by the car in front, they are not much good. We are therefore giving a version based upon the Highway Code, but with the additions that are nowadays essential.

Hey for the Open Road.

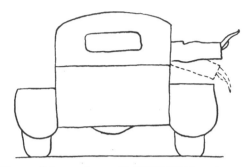

No. 1.   " I am going to SLOW DOWN, or STOP."

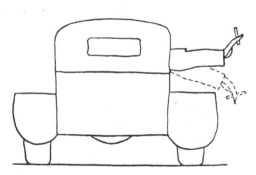

No. 1a.   " I am going to shake the ash off my
CIGARETTE."

10

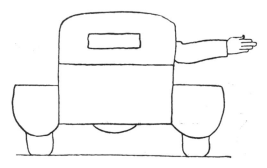

No. 2.   " I am going to TURN to my RIGHT."

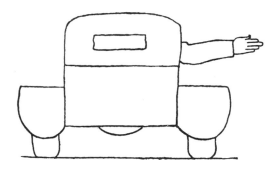

No. 2a.   "I am going to TURN to my RIGHT,
and when I discover that it 's the wrong turning,
I am going to TURN BACK again just in time
to give you the FRIGHT of your LIFE."

11

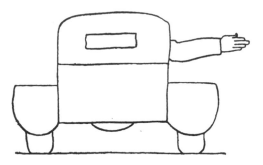

No. 2b.　" The rain is OFF, I think."

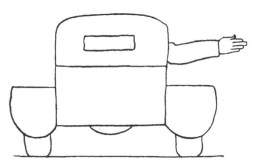

No. 2c.　" The house over there with the GREEN
door is where our cook's MOTHER lives."

12

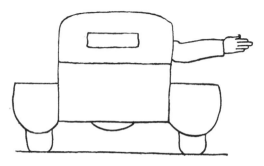

No. 2d. " LOOK, I can drive with one HAND off
the WHEEL."

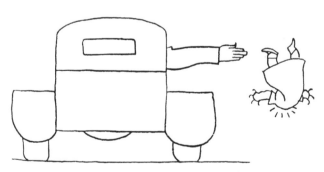

No. 2e. " By JOVE, there goes BABY."

13

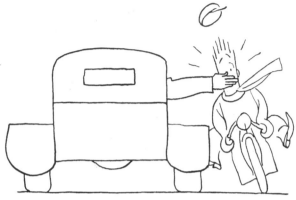

No. 2f.   " Take THAT, you BRUTE."

Signal No. 3: "I am READY to be OVER-TAKEN," is omitted and the following, which has virtually superseded it, is put in instead:

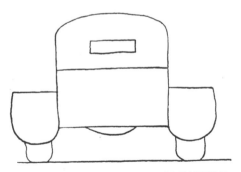

No. 3a.   " I will NOT be OVERTAKEN."

14

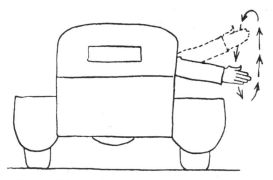

No. 4.   ". I am going to TURN to my LEFT."

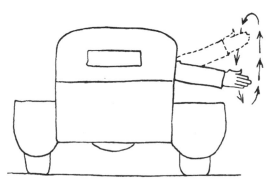

No. 4a.   " My ARM 'S got PINS and NEEDLES."

Now we come to the drivers of HORSE-DRAWN vehicles, who have a section all to themselves. Their signals are as follows:

No. 5. " I am going to STOP."

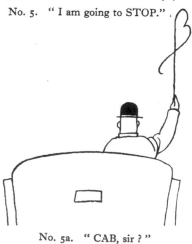

No. 5a. " CAB, sir ? "

No. 5b. " I am just going to TRY a couple of CASTS."

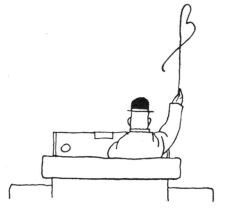

No. 5c. " I am FRIGHTFULLY fond of HORSES."

17

No. 5d.   " I have disregarded the Ministry's instruction to
keep the WHIP clear of other TRAFFIC."

No. 6.   " I am going to TURN."

18

No. 6a.   " Hip, hip, HOORAY."

No. 6b.   " My God, I've grown TWO right ARMS."

Signals 7, 8 and 9, which complete the code, are described as signals by drivers to police constables. For drivers who obey the spirit of the code, they

" Well, what about swapping cars ? "

should not, we feel, be necessary, any more than those frequently used by drivers to express their personal opinion of other drivers. The only really fitting gesture from the average driver to a point-duty policeman is that of raising the hat. (In the case of A.A. and R.A.C. scouts, moreover, it would usually be much more fitting if the motorist did the saluting.)

It will be noticed that so far nothing has been said about the signals made by mechanical and electrical devices. A complete range of these is therefore given opposite.

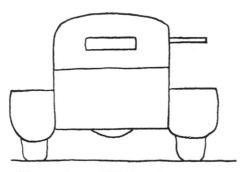

No. 10. " I am going to TURN to the RIGHT," or " I am
going to STOP," or " I am going to SLOW down," or " I am
going to TURN round," or " SEE, I press this thing, and UP it
comes."

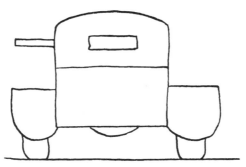

No. 11. " I am going to TURN to the LEFT."

21

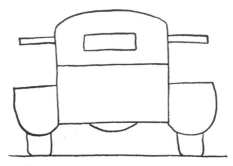

No. 12. " I am going to have it put RIGHT to-morrow."

Finally, a few signals, which, though not part of any definite system or plan, are nevertheless frequently seen.

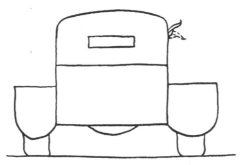

No. 13. " I am going to TURN to the LEFT or the RIGHT or SLOW down or SKID or STOP or maybe DASH across and ask the WAY from the policeman on POINT duty."

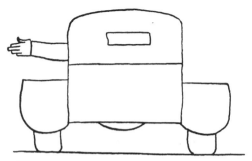

No. 14. " I am going to STAY with Aunt
EMILY to-morrow."

No. 15. " I am going to SHOUT for HELP."

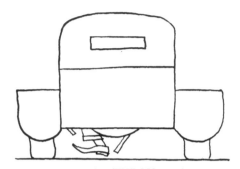

No. 16. " I am going THROUGH the FLOOR."

No. 17. " I think I am going to be SICK."

24

No. 18. " I have just been MARRIED."

No. 19. " I have just REVERSED into something."

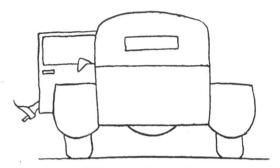

No. 20.   " I have just been INSULTED."

No. 21.   " I have just filled up with OIL."

Special Sections

(a) Lorries.

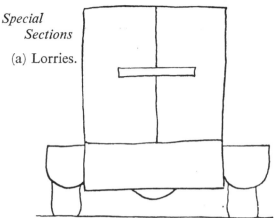

No. 22. " I am going to CONTINUE in the middle of the road for another FIVE miles."

No. 23. " You may OVERTAKE me on my RIGHT: it is all clear in front except for TWO BUSES, a TRACTION ENGINE, a NARROW bridge and three CYCLISTS round a blind CORNER."

No. 24. " I am a VERY RUDE boy."

(b) Push bicycles.

No. 25. " I am going to keep WELL in to the LEFT
side of the road."

28

No. 25a. "I am going to SWERVE suddenly out into the MIDDLE of the road, and, with LUCK, back again."

No. 26. "I am going to appear suddenly from NOWHERE, and dash STRAIGHT across the road with a basket of GROCERIES on my handle-bars."

29

(c) Motor bicycles.

No. 27. " I am going to REMAIN on the carrier."

No. 27a. " I am NOT going to REMAIN on the carrier."

(d) Pedestrians.

No. 28. " Run over me if you DARE."

No. 29. " Run over me if you LIKE."

31

No. 30. " I am going to wait till the light goes GREEN and then step slowly off the pavement."

No. 31. " I'm in urgent need of HELP."

No. 31a.   " I'm a car BANDIT."

33

" Sorry, but I'm a stranger here."

SECTION III

TAKING ROUTE

" Up the airy mountain, down the rushy glen."

**Famous
Last Words**

"Come on, Mabel,
there's plenty
more room on
the carrier."

ONCE upon a time the process of taking the road was quite an adventure, and was preceded by complicated preliminaries. Nowadays, of course, it is quite a commonplace, and similar to every other phase of our daily existence. In other words one merely has to

(a) fill up forms and send them with the appropriate sum to the County Council.
(b) fill up forms and send them with the appropriate sum to the insurance company.
(c) fill up forms and send them with the appropriate sum to the Supervising Examiner (Driving Tests).
(d) fill up forms and send them with the appropriate sum to the County Council (Driving Licence).

Won by a neck.

For (a), (b) and (d) only the usual skill is necessary; (c), however, entails an examination as to your fitness to drive (unless you were born on the 1st April, 1934). This examination would seem to offer certain difficulties—that is to say, you naturally cannot

undergo an examination as to your skill in driving until you have had considerable experience in handling a car on the high road. On the other hand, you equally naturally must not drive a car on the high road until you have been examined and declared to be a safe person to do so.

However, a compromise has been arrived at. The learner-driver fixes a large "L" to his car, and, with this, he may push off into the traffic and bump along with impunity until finally he takes his rightful place in the stream.

The supply of "L" cars is the difficulty. It is impractical to learn in one's own car and pretty difficult to learn in any one else's. The solution lies in the various Schools of Driving: and that is why, in practically every "L" car that you meet, you find two people. One of them is calm, self-assured and perfectly confident of his ability to handle any situation. The other is nervous, jumpy and scared stiff. The latter, of course, is the instructor.

" Sorry, but I'm a stranger here."

SECTION IV

ROADS SCHOLARSHIP

" I will arise and go now, and go to Innisfree."

𝔉amous
𝔏ast 𝔚ords

" I love the early
morning—the roads
are so empty."

As already mentioned, intending drivers have to undergo an examination.

It is not, however, generally known that in addition to a practical driving test candidates have to do a written paper.

In view of this, and for the benefit of readers who are sitting for their finals we give below a specimen paper with appropriate answers attached.

EXAMINATION

Parking Limit—Two Hours.
Write on one side of the road only.

(a) *Mechanics*

1. Your car, except for a tendency to slow down on hills, runs perfectly all day.

   On starting it up next morning, however, you find that it will only move a few inches. What would you do?

Answer : Open the garage door.

2. Why is a hand pump included in the tool-kit?

Answer: It gives employment.

(b) *History*

1. Describe the difference between roads made by the Romans and those constructed nowadays.

Answer: The roads made by the Romans have lasted until the present time.

(c) *English Grammar*

1. What is wrong with the following: "When I got to the crossroads I hooted and slowed down and looked to see was it safe to cross"?

Answer: It isn't true.

2. What is the feminine of khaki shorts?

Answer: Too tight.

3. "I have just done a month for having no third-party insurance." What is wrong with the above sentence?

Answer: Not long enough.

(d) *General Knowledge*

1. Why is a red light used for danger?

Answer: Because a bright colour that cannot be confused with anything else is essential.

2. Why is a red light used for advertising restaurants, cinemas, drinks, shops, pills and everything else?

Answer: See above.

3. Why does a car ferry require a crew of two?

Answer: One to say " whoa " while the other says " come on."

4. What is the yellow traffic light for?

Answer: To save waiting for the green.

(e) *Legal*

1. What vehicles are allowed to drive at high speed on either side of the road, across any traffic lights and both ways along one-way streets?

Answer: Those driven by very charming young ladies.

2. A motorist comes suddenly out of a small
   side road, dashes straight across a main
   line of traffic against the lights, mounts the
   pavement, runs right up the steps of a public-
   house, crashes through the door and finally
   comes to rest hard up against the bar. Is
   he liable for damages?

Answer : No, not unless he has his car with him.

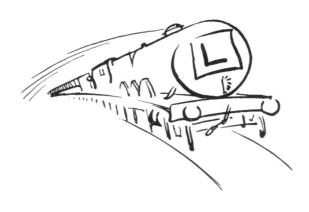

SECTION V

SOUND ENGINEERING

" In the highlands, in the country places."

**Famous
Last Words**

" I've ridden bikes
for years and never
had a light."

SOUND ENGINEERING

FOR the tyro, the purchase of a car is not only one of the first steps—it is also one of the easiest. All makers of repute now produce cars that will do absolutely everything that you can possibly want with effortless ease: moreover, they also produce cheaper models that will do absolutely everything that you can possibly want.

At the same time different requirements naturally call for different types.

For instance, if you want an all-purpose dependable family car with a great deal of engineering experience behind it, but no frills, we would recommend the *Kingston Rattlesnake*, of which the maker's specification is as follows:

"*Once more Spring's dainty fingers are waking the woods from their winter slumber. Once more the thoughts of the motorist turn with yearning to the countryside, and to the joys that only a RATTLESNAKE can bestow.*"

Park de Triomphe.

" I always say to them—' Well, why do you want
to go fast ? ' "

Of course, if you wish for something more dashing
—for a car more suited to the jeunesse dorée or
platinée—then you will find the *Byfleet Polecat*
nearer to your requirements. The maker's descrip-
tion is worth quoting in full:

"*Once more Spring's dainty fingers are waking
the woods from their winter slumber. Once more
the thoughts of the motorist turn with yearning
to the countryside, and to the joys that only a
POLECAT can bestow.*"

It may be, again, that you live among the hills,
and therefore need a
design that gives ample
reserve of power with
exceptional strength of
construction. In this
case, you cannot do
better than to invest in
a *Hampstead Vampire*.
The technical details of
its design speak for
themselves:

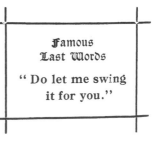

𝕱amous
𝕷ast 𝔚ords

" Do let me swing
it for you."

*"Once more Spring's dainty fingers are waking
the woods from their winter slumber. Once more
the thoughts of the motorist turn with yearning
to the countryside, and to the joys that only a
VAMPIRE can bestow."*

There are many other cars, of course, each of
them designed to meet some special engineering
problem, but enough should have been said by now:
study the advertisements, compare the technical details and select two or three types that split the

". . . holds the road better than any car I've had."

difference most hopefully between what you want
and what you want to pay.

You can then, if you wish, ask all your friends for
their opinions. It should be remembered, however,
that owners are apt to be misleading as to actual
performance.

For instance, if you ask A, who is the owner of
a large dull saloon, upholstered with some clinging
velvety material, he will probably say: "It's a very
sound job, and it suits me quite well."

On the other hand, if you approach young B,

51

who spends most of his time fitting new and comparatively big ends to his supercharged straight eight, he will probably tell you: "It suits me quite well—it's a very sound job."

C, again, who has a tiny baby car that lives in the larder, will almost undoubtedly answer: "It's a very sound job," while D, who owns several cars of various makes (but has given up motoring because his own version of the new regulations confuses him so) will probably say of any one of them: "Well, it suits *me* very well."

Finally, having made your decision, go to your niece's young man in the trade and tell him what you have chosen. In due course you will find yourself the proud possessor of a car—although, as he is not an agent for that particular make, it will not be quite the one you chose.

BRIC-À-BRAC

" Under yonder beech-tree single on the green-sward."

Famous
Last Words

" Quick, that's our
turning."

SINCE the early days of motoring there have been many changes in the apparatus designed to keep drivers posted as to any sensational developments under the bonnet. In the first cars there was little or none of this form of affectation. If you smelt burning you suspected that the engine might be running hot and when your feet burst into flames your impressions were confirmed. Oil pressure, if any, was usually taken for granted. If the engine seized it was fair to assume that the oil pressure had not come up to expectations. If the oil pipes burst, it was equally fair to assume that it had.

The temperature of the water in the radiator was a parallel case. Steam coming out of the radiator, as elsewhere, indicated that the water was boiling, and a radiator that slowly became incandescent showed that it had finished doing so. That was about all there was to go on—just a few fundamentals

" A Jack, sir ? Do you mean a Knave ? "

upon which the motorist had to base all his deductions. In those days motorists *were* motorists. Nowadays things are made so easy for them that they cavil at having to carry out the simplest roadside repair, such as slipping in a new crank-shaft—or even removing the body to fit a new dash-light.

The history of the dashboard is interesting. From its humble beginning as the thing that kept the two

" Get off the road ! "

sides of the car from falling apart, it rapidly became the centre of interest. This encouraged the experts to persevere until they had evolved every instrument that could possibly convey any sort of anxiety to the mind of the driver. The Art Departments then took a hand, and transformed the pleasantly messy looking collection of dials thus produced into a matched set of modern shapes in pastel shades that brought joy to the heart of the prospective lady driver, although it made the real old-timer feel terrible.

As a result, the lady driver (and very often her car) has of recent years progressed by leaps and bounds.

In view of this, and as a help to her, we now give

in simple language a general guide to the various complications that she may from time to time discover in or near the instrument board.

1. *Oil Gauge*

This is a little clock with "Pounds per square inch" on its face. It has only one hand, which moons vaguely about. A sudden return to zero can mean a hundred different things to the expert, but never more than one to the beginner, who won't have noticed anything anyway.

" Get off the road ! "

2. *Speedometer*

This is another and slightly larger clock, also with one hand. It is linked up with the wheels in some way, and the original idea was that when you were doing 40 miles per hour the hand pointed to 40. Nowadays speeds have increased so much that when the hand points to 80 you are doing 60, and when it points to 10 you are probably in reverse.

3. *Radiator Temperature*

A great many cars have got a little device which tells you if the water in your radiator is too hot. If it keeps on pointing to boiling, you need a new fan belt, or a new radiator, or a new engine, or else a new little device.

E

4. *Ammeter*

This is for measuring electricity and is easily recognized, being the only dial that has nought in the middle, and scores both above and below the line.

It is the most picturesque means of knowing if your battery is discharging—but not the most usual.

5. *Free Wheel*

This is a clever device which allows a car to stop

" Get off the road ! "

pedalling like a bicycle. It has great advantages for those motorists who insist on getting into low gear when descending a steep hill, since, by means of this device, they can do so without any loss of speed whatever.

6. *Rev. Counter*

This, in spite of its name, is a purely · secular instrument. It tells you how fast your engine is going, and, if you watch it carefully enough, you can change gear absolutely noiselessly—apart from the tinkling of glass as you drive through a shop window in the process.

58

7. *Clock*

This is just the same as any ordinary clock, except that it always points to ten-past seven.

8. *Synchro-mesh*

This is just a 'whimsy.' The idea is that you make it awfully easy to make one change, and frightfully difficult to make the next. Thus you satisfy not only the driver who likes to say: "I bet you can't hear this change" but also the candid

" Get off the road ! "

friend who likes to answer: "Yes, I did."

9. *Traffic Indicators*

The idea behind these gadgets is to tell people when you are turning, or have just turned, to the right or left. This is usually done by a little switch on the wheel or the dashboard. In earlier days they could be relied upon to make frequent and most dramatic contributions to the pageantry of the road. Nowadays, of course, they are all fool-proof, and many of them are small-boy-proof as well.

10. *Lamp Switches*

These are very simple. The first position puts on

59

the side and tail lights and the next position puts them out. The next again turns on the headlights, and the one after that produces a smell of burning rubber. The last position dips the headlights, and after a year or two, starts up the horn. The position that fuses the tail light is not known, as you don't

" Get off the road ! "

find it out until later.

11. *Ignition Switches*

These vary tremendously. Some you pull out, some you slide, some you push in, and a great many you have to unlock. As keys are apt to be mislaid, a first-class car thief should be included in the tool-kit.

12. *Gear Levers*

A gear lever used to be an important part of the car. In a real man's car it was sometimes necessary to use both hands and one foot braced against a window to get it into position. Nowadays the gears have either little toy levers, like teaspoons, or else long and willowy levers, like bulrushes, that bend and quiver rather charmingly in the slightest breeze.

13. *Throttles*

Foot throttles still have the carnival spirit, and if pedestrians only knew that one's last car had the brake outside the throttle and one's new car has not, they would use the subways whenever possible.

" Get off the road ! "

14. *Hand Brake*

This is, in theory, a sort of safety device to be grabbed at in an emergency. Actually it is often found under the seat or the dashboard, and takes anything up to three quarters of an hour to grab at.

15. *Choke*

The choke is a relic of the time when a run of any distance was in the nature of a war to the death between the man and the machine. It was in those days the final awful threat that the driver held over his engine. To-day it is merely a thing to be pulled out when starting, or when trying to run without petrol.

And that is about all the instruments on the average car. There are, of course, many other complications, such as automatic switches, which make the engine switch itself on whenever it stops, and have made a great many old-fashioned motorists swear the car's haunted: and there are many exquisite refinements such as fluid fly-wheels and self-changing gears, which tend to convert motoring into a sedentary occupation. In fairness to all concerned, it should be said that the average car to-day goes with such absurd regularity that the instrument board is of purely academic interest. That is possibly why car radio sets are becoming so popular.

" Get off the road ! "

" Sorry, but I'm a stranger here."

LE TOURING

" Now sleeps the crimson petal, now the white."

Famous
Last Words

" Thanks, I can light my own— this car steers itself."

No tour can compare with the first—not at the time, that is. The planning of the route, the packing and repacking, the rise at dawn in order to get off early, and finally the start at lunch-time, make up an experience that remains in the memory long after the marks made by the luggage are forgotten.

There are two ways of setting about it. The first is to request one of the large motoring organizations to provide a complete itinerary, and those that prefer this method probably cannot do better than to request one of the large motoring organizations to provide a complete itinerary. This will undoubtedly make it so pleasant and simple that they will hardly realize they have left home.

" O waly, waly, up the bank."

The more enterprising and ridiculous method is to work it out for oneself, and for this all that is necessary is a good guide-book.

" Whoa."

As, however, the average work of this nature contains too much information in some directions and too little in others, we give in the following pages a model guide-book, which overcomes at least one of these difficulties. It consists, as is customary, of two parts, as follows:

Part I. Gazetteer, containing details of all towns and villages in Great Britain.

Guide-books usually give a detailed list of every single town and village, with a plan of every sizable town. This, as every road-user knows, is nowadays quite unnecessary, as virtually every town presents the same obstacles to those passing through it, or even staying for the night. We therefore only give the useful details of one town (with accompanying plan) and one village (without one).

As regards hotels, we feel that the usual grading

from one star up to five is somewhat inadequate·
We have therefore expanded the classifications as
follows:

Five stars represent luxuriously appointed palaces,
of such size that every comfort may be looked
for, and many of them discovered.

" I shall only pass this way but once."

69

Four stars represent well-appointed and comfortable hotels, with modern improvements.

Three stars represent comfortable hotels with modern improvements under repair.

Two stars represent hotels that are under entirely new management.

One star represents small hotels that are simple but clean.

One blot represents small hotels that are simple.

Two blots represent slightly larger hotels with hearts in the right place—and everything else in the wrong one.

Three blots represent really uncomfortable medium-sized hotels, half-timbered outside and even less inside.

Four blots represent gaily-coloured chromium and
wicker hotels, built entirely for speed and not
for comfort.

Five blots represent vast barracks with every dis-
comfort that man can produce with the aid of
lard, dumb waiters, mattresses filled with fire-
wood, and special terms to the wrong people.

" I didn't know they were dangerous."

71

EVERYTOWN.

Population—mostly in middle of street.

Parking Places—full.

Market Day—to-day.

Licensing Hours—yes.

Post—midday to-morrow.

Early Closing—remarkably.

See—John Gilpin Memorial Park, John Gilpin Museum, John Gilpin Art Gallery, Roman Baths, Gilpin & Co.'s Glue Factory.

Hotels

☆ ☆ ☆   County, 53 brms, 4 bth, B 3/-, L 3/6, D 5/-, R. 8/- to 18/-.
Tel: Comfort.

☆   King's Head, 6 brms, 1 bth, B 2/6, L 3/-, H.T. 2/6, R. 6/- to 12/-.
Tel: Welcome.

🔔 🔔 🔔   Norman Close, 65 brms, 2 bth, C & C, B 3/6, L 4/-, D 6/6, R. 10/- to 20/-.
Tel: Domesday.

🔔 🔔 🔔 🔔 🔔   Magnificent, 300 brms, 299 bth, H & C. B 5/-, L 10/-, D 15/-, R. 20/- and upwards.
Tel: Blondin.

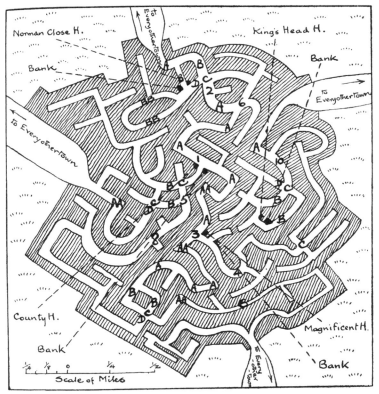

EVERYTOWN

PLAN

Dang. Corners. A

Worse Dang. Corners. A A

Dang. Sight worse still. A A A

One-way street—B

Hardly that—B B

Main crossroads—C

Main crossroads with concealed or misleading signposts or none at all—C

Concealed Traffic signals—D

Note : All streets cobbled and tramlined

EVERYVILLAGE

Population —at the Wagoner's Arms.

Parking Places —both sides of the street, where narrow (residents only).

Licensing Hours—no.

Post —send a wire.

See —Manor House (Queen Elizabeth's bed), 12th century Church (fee), Devil's Leap, Devil's Punch-bowl, Devil's Bridge, Devil's Own Dangerous Crossroads.

Hotels

The Wagoner's Arms, 1 brm, B 2/6, L 2/6, D 2/6, R. 5/- to 5/-, Ch. 10/-.

The Ploughman's Arms, ditto.

The Suspected Poacher's Arms, ditto.

The Gardener's Daughter's Arms, ditto.

"The Hog's Back."
"I didn't know he'd been away."

74

" I wonder if it's cured that squeak."

(B) *Maps*

Here, again, it used to be the custom to plan one's route from X to Y by the most direct roads. A complete set of maps was therefore imperative.

Nowadays, of course, it is realized that distance counts for little, and that the main causes of delay are imperfect roads and *slowing down to read signposts*. Thus the wise motorist, instead of spending unneces-

𝔉amous
𝔏ast 𝔚ords

" I always just walk across, like this."

75

sary time (a) studying the map, and (b) trying to put the result of such study into practice, now simply proceeds along the mainest road in the required direction; when he gets somewhere near, he asks the way. And so no maps are required, and therefore none are included here, save the one on the next page. This is merely put in to show what a bird's-eye view of the country would look like to a bird of rather more than average intelligence.

Map showing distances representing an easy day's run from Hyde Park Corner, in various directions.

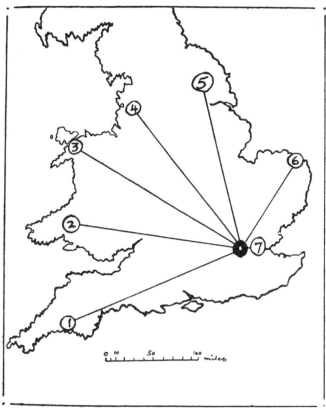

1. Plymouth	4. Wigan
2. Carmarthen	5. York
3. Carnarvon	6. Cromer

7. Aldgate, E.

" Sorry, but I'm a stranger here."

SECTION VIII

IN TOWN TO-NIGHT

" Season of mists and mellow fruitfulness ! "

**Famous
Last Words**

" Look, here's the
thousand just
coming up."

PRACTICALLY the only difference between driving in London and parking in London is that you may not park on the same spot for more than two hours at a stretch.

For this and other reasons, cars are hardly used at all during the day, but much more hardly used at night. All the same, it is often difficult to decide whether or not to use your own car, when dining out or going to a theatre.

Without your car, you have, of course, the expense of taxis (although the fact that you live nearer to the centre than the fellow-guest you have invited to share your taxi home may possibly reduce the cost).

With your car, however, you have to

(a) miss half the first act while parking, and probably most of the point

(b)   pay tip or fine or both

(c)   run down battery, and worry all the evening if she'll start

(d)   take fellow-guest to Southgate, because it sounded like South Ken

and

(e) add petrol, oil and depreciation. (This last should not be a serious item, and probably no more than twice the cost of taxis.)

SECTION IX

ACHTUNG À DROITE

" The year 's at the spring."

Famous
Last Words

" . . . every inch
of this road."

MOTORING abroad is exactly the same as motoring at home, except that

(a) instead of driving on the left you drive on the right

(b) instead of cornering on two wheels you corner on one

(c) instead of sticking your arm out to signal your intentions you pull it in

(d) instead of going over crossroads when you know it's safe you know it's safe when you go over them

DEFENSE DE DOUBLER

(e) instead of doing so many miles to the gallon you do so few to the litre

(f) instead of hitting a telegraph pole you hit a tree

and

(g) you hoot at level crossings.

SECTION X

DEA IN MACHINA

" Under the greenwood tree."

Famous
Last Words

"If you brake carefully, worn tyres don't matter a bit."

THE awful fag of changing. The silliness of being social. The fantastic idea of going twenty-five miles just for a dance. The way a white tie suddenly wilts.

The awful stupidity of locking and bolting garages the moment before a fellow wants to get his car out. The agony of a bumper in the dark. The foul nuisance of keeping a car at all.

The irritation of sitting on new tails. The devilish way that batteries run down. The curse of an engine that simply will not start. The torture of backing a car in the dark when you're wearing a razor-edged evening collar.

The nasty twang of a wing on a door post. The awful plague of an engine that splutters for

" That's petrol, that was."

ages after starting up. The lunatic who hasn't heard of concealed drives.

The muck people talk about the pleasures of motoring. Those blinding headlights. The foul manners of every other motorist. The absurd way roads wind about.

The hopeless dimness of your headlights compared with every one else's. The thought that you might be just going to bed to read in comfort,

The way the moon makes your lights seem feebler still. The awful bilge people talk about the moon. The wickedness of hump-backed bridges. The car's revolting lack of acceleration. The steadily increasing number of cars driving like mad. The arrival in the car park. The absurd fussiness of some idiots about their wings.

The final tweak at the white tie.

The dance itself.

*　　*　　*　　*　　*

The exquisite vision of loveliness.

*　　*　　*　　*　　*

The hesitating offer of a lift. The astounding fact of its acceptance. The bounding on air to get the car.

The perfect way the engine starts.

The absolute ecstasy of driving at night.

The happy song of the engine. The staggering loveliness of the open road by moonlight. The exquisite tracery of the trees against the sky. The joy of a road that curves and twists so light-heartedly. The glorious green of the grass in the headlights.

The lovely flying feeling when you take a humped-back bridge in your stride.

The glorious scent of new-mown hay. The cheerful smell of cowsheds.

The wonderful joys that the car has brought to mankind. The inspiring rush of the wind. The perfectly marvellous view over the gas-works.

The exquisite magic of the moonlight.

The happy thrill of meeting wandering cows. The pleasant warmth from the engine. The fine reassuring smell of hot oil. The joy of communing with nature. The glory of the first glimmer of the dawn.

The regret that she doesn't live at Land's End. The final good night. The joy of singing while you drive. The jolly bump as you reach the far end of the garage. The solid peace when you switch off the engine. The friendly greeting of the bumper as you pass.

The truly laughable discovery that you have lost your key.

" Sorry, but I'm a stranger here."

SECTION XI

ROADHOGMANAY

" It was the time of roses—we pluck'd
them as we pass'd ! "

Famous Last Words

" You really must
look at that
sunset."

. . . OF course most of the trouble on the roads
would be avoided if people would only cultivate a
sense of proportion and stop driving much too fast
in the hopes of saving five minutes that they don't
know what to do with when they've saved them and
then they would be able to drive a perfectly beautiful
machine along a perfectly wonderful road in perfect
peace and toleration as I'm doing now instead of
thinking they've got to roar about and hoot and risk
every one's lives by cutting in like that fellow in the
blue car in front which only makes them get into a
filthy state of nerves over anything likely to hinder
their foul progress like that madman who's just

" Where's George ? "

95

passed and if they only realized it they'd get there just as quickly and easily if they took it perfectly calmly as I'm doing or anyhow they would if only the ridiculous way they go on didn't hinder every one else like this blithering idiot who's just turned right across us and if half-baked louts like this man just in front didn't glue themselves to the crown of the road and make one hoot at them till one's completely deaf and if half-witted pedestrians like that one didn't simply hurl themselves under the wheels whenever we appeared suddenly round a bend, and if this type of lorry-driving fiend didn't lumber about the roads hiding everything in front so that one has just got to trust blindly to luck every time one cuts in front of them on a corner and if absolute raving lunatics like this one didn't hurtle at full speed along a main road quite oblivious of the fact that we might be dashing suddenly out of a side road at the same moment and if everything else on the road didn't take a perfectly hellish delight in getting in one's way and making one lose precious minutes and blast you will you get out of my—CRASH TWANG TINKLE BUMP . . . !

CORRESPONDENCE COLUMN

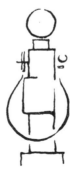

" Piping down the valleys wild."

Famous
Last Words

"At last, darling."

CORRESPONDENCE COLUMN

O woman, in our hours of ease,
Uncertain, coy and hard to please,
What pain and anguish wring the brow,
Whene'er you say " I'll take her now ! "

I

MY DARLING ANGELA,
My dear, guess what has happened.
Daddy has actually promised to give me a car, and
I am so excited I can hardly spell. Anyway, what
I want to know is—as you know all about them
will you please advise me about choosing one. I
think I ought to have a fairly small one, preferably
grey with red leather seats, because of that dress I
got that day, but I'll be guided by you entirely, as
you're the *only person in the world I can really trust*
and every one says you have to be awfully careful
when buying a car. Above all I want a good gear.
A girl near here has what she calls a sports car,
and she says the trouble with it is you have to keep
on changing the gears. Do you think you could
be an angel and tell me of some kind of car that
has got one really good gear that will go on for
about a year without having to be changed? I
think that would be simply perfect.
I have only once tried to drive and I feel
rather strongly that a car with some sort of bumper
would be best; as you know, the people round here
are very old-fashioned. I suppose you heard that
Henry never married that girl after all. Mrs. T. was

perfectly speechless with fury for months, but I must say that we all laughed like a row of buckets.

Another thing is going backwards. Our garage has only got one door at present, so I suppose I had better have a car that can go both ways; I believe they nearly all do.

I know the Doctor's goes backwards quite marvellously. His small boy drove it last night right into the orchard. You simply must come and stay with us next month, the fruit is simply marvellous, and Mummy has got three first prizes for marrows—or rather, a marrow.

The only other thing is miles per gallon. Daddy says this is frightfully important so perhaps we had better have some.

I must stop now,

With love,

PRUDENCE.

PS. It must be small, because the roads here are so narrow and full of buses, and it must hold four people comfortably because of the dogs and parcels and things.

II

DEAREST PRUDENCE,

I know exactly the very car you want—
it is a 20-litre two-seater sports Tornado. It has
just about enough power for what you want, and
as for reliability, it has done over 100,000 miles
since it was overhauled in 1922. Its present colour
is primrose and it has its name, "The Yellow Streak,"
painted on the side, but you could have it re-done
any colour you like, and of course a hood could
easily be fixed on somewhere.

You would simply love it, I know, and the price
to you, darling, will be very reasonable indeed. I
will drive it over to-morrow if I can, but it may be
the next day as it's been in our garage for some
time now and may want something done before it
will start. I'm so thrilled to think that you're
really going to have it.

All my love,

Your ANGELA.

101

" Sorry, but I'm a stranger here."

REMOTE CONTROL

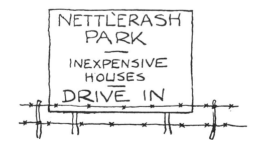

"What have I done for you, England, my England?"

Famous
Last Words

"It's all right, she's
not in gear."

"YES, darling, the tank's quite full.

"Yes, there's oil on the steering wheel, so I think he must have.

"Yes, darling, I'm quite ready to start—I was only waiting for you and the children. Don't you trouble, darling, *I'll* shut the door—and the other door—ah, and this one, too.

"Yes, darling, I saw him coming—that's why I didn't hit him, darling. No, I didn't hoot because I could see there wasn't anything coming—anyway, there wasn't anything coming when I didn't hoot, darling—no, I *will* be careful, darling. I don't think this is the short cut, darling—I don't think it can be quite as short as this, this is a blind alley, darling.

"No, darling, I didn't know I was reversing into a lamp-post. I thought *you* were looking, darling— no, I didn't think you had eyes in the back of your

H 105

head—I was prepared to bet you hadn't—no, darling, I didn't say anything.

"Very well, darling, I'll look out for a post office—I'm sorry but that one was on the wrong side of the

road—also it was a Bank, darling—but here's one, darling—well, it *calls* itself a post office, darling—Oh, I see, you want a telephone box, darling. No, darling, not that one unless you want to talk to Scotland Yard, the telephone ones aren't blue, darling, they're red—like this one. No, darling, you can't use it at the same time as some one else—I told you so, darling—I'm sorry, I thought you heard —anyway, I thought you knew, darling. He's gone now, darling—very well then, leave the door open, darling, or smoke yourself—no, darling, I haven't a shilling, a sixpence and three pennies—I've got half a crown, if you care to send love and best wishes to make up the difference.

"Now, off we go—I said off we go, darling—no darling, I didn't mean I was tired of waiting, I only meant off we go. Very well, darling, we'll lunch early—no, darling, it isn't in front here—is it that big yellow basket? Ah, then, I know where it is —no, darling, I'm afraid it's not all right, it's in the front hall—no, darling, I didn't say it was all right. I said I knew where it was, but not what it was,

darling—if I'd known, I'd have brought it, darling, even if it had turned out to be the washing. No, darling, the washing isn't here. I'm sorry, darling, it's the row the children are making. Yes, darling, of course we'll stop and buy some—yes, darling, I'll keep a look-out as we go through the town—

sorry, darling, I missed it—I was busy dodging those trams, darling—but here's one, darling. Certainly, darling, we'll go on to another one. I didn't see the dust in the back of the shop, darling, I was dazzled by the traffic lights—no, darling, that's not sarcasm,

that's hyperbole—nothing, darling—what, darling? —so sorry, darling, but I couldn't stop there with that bus behind and the policeman waving me on, darling. Very well, darling, next time I'll just wave back."

"How about this one, darling?—or this one, then?—or that one?—I'm afraid we're getting away from the shops now, darling—— Well, try that paper shop then, darling—even if it can't give you lunch, it can give you something to wrap it up in—— Why not go to the back door of this house and beg, darling? 'Sorry ,darling, I wasn't trying to be funny, I meant beg like a dog, darling. Ah, here's a garage place open all night—and shut all day, apparently— no, it's all right, here's some one. Right, darling,

I'll look for somewhere to lunch. That's too shady, is it, darling?—and this is too sunny?—and that's too near that house?—and that's too near that

pond?—and this looks too like a bog?—and that looks too like a bull?—— Yes, darling, I do know it's after four and that we mustn't be *too* particular.

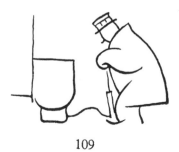

Here, darling?—well, no one could call us too particular here, darling!—yes, darling, I know it's only for a short time, and we'll soon get used to it—yes, darling, it's the local rubbish dump, I can see

a notice—are you quite comfortable, or shall I move those tins a bit?

"Ah, it's fresher now we're moving again—yes, darling, I know the time's getting on—I'll go as fast as I can, darling—sorry, darling—I'll go as slow as I can, darling—yes, darling—no, darling—no, darling—yes, darling—what, darling?—— Of course, darling—no, darling—certainly, darling—so here we are at last, darling. Yes, darling—I'll take all the stuff in, darling—what's that, darling?—the children's coats are left at the place where we lunched ?

No, darling, I didn't speak, darling."

EXCELSIORLITTLEBYLITTLE

" A garden is a lovesome thing, God wot ! "

Famous
Last Words

" He's gaining—I
can see him in
the mirror."

EXCELSIORLITTLEBYLITTLE

1.

JNO. FETLOCK
Shoeing Smith

2.

JNO. FETLOCK
Blacksmith
Bicycles Repaired

3.

JOHN FETLOCK
Cycle & Motor Repairer

4.

J. FETLOCK & SON
Motor Agent

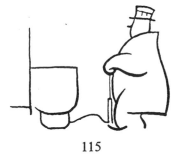

5.

J. FETLOCK & SONS
Motor Engineers
Petrol & Oil

6.

J. FETLOCK & CO.
Automobile Engineers
Teas & Minerals

7.

J. FETLOCK & CO.
Automobile Service Engineers
Good Pull in for drivers
Snacks

8.

J. FETLOCK & CO.
Free Air
Café open all night

9.

FETLOCK & CO., LTD.
Garage Proprietors
Restaurant
Chauffeurs' Room at Rear

𝔉amous
𝔏ast 𝔚ords

"Anyway, the hand-
brake's all right, I
think."

116

10.

FETLOCK'S MOTORS, LTD.
Restaurant
Dancing
No Charabancs

11.

YE MERRIE ENGLAND
(Fetlock's Motors, Ltd.)
Dancing
Dinner 3/6
Bathing Pool
Car Park

12.

CHATEAU D'AMOUR
Diner dansant
Cabaret
Poule de Bain
Fully Licensed

SECTION XV

CAME THE DAWN — A FRAGMENT

" Ye flowery banks o' bonnie Doon."

Famous
Last Words

" No   one   ever
makes *me* dim
my headlights."

"I was pressed for time, and I suppose I drove a bit faster than usual. At all events, as I was approaching the crossroads, a large traction-engine with a van attached steamed majestically out of the lane on the left and I had the choice of taking the van or the ditch. . . .

*　　*　　*　　*　　*

"As I climbed ruefully out of my car, a fellow drew up in a smart-looking two-seater.

"'Do you want any help?' said he.

"'Not for the car, thanks awfully,' I said, 'that can wait in the ditch till I send to yank it out—but for myself, if you're going near a station, I'd be eternally grateful for a lift.'

"'Of course,' he said, 'get in.'

"We went up an unfamiliar turning, and along a

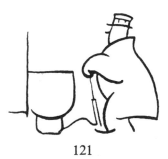

road that became more and more remarkable. On either side were, strangely enough, endless beds of flowers, with trees behind for shelter while the road

itself had the pleasing mellow tone of a Gloucestershire farmhouse. I remarked on it to my good Samaritan.

"'Yes,' he said, 'that's Mark II.'

"'Mark II?' I inquired, 'what's that?'

"'Mark II surface,' he explained, 'is the one with little longitudinal furrows, exactly the same as the standard tyre tread. It gives minimum resistance to travel and maximum to skid. In the old days, as maybe you remember, all the tyre manufacturers tried to produce a tyre to suit every surface and all the road experts tried to make a surface to suit every sort of tyre. It wasn't until road surface and tyre-tread were designed together that skidding really ceased.'

"'Ceased?' I said. 'Well, since you're so kind as to drive me to the station, I won't question your statement. If this is Mark II, what's Mark I?'

"'Mark I,' he answered, 'is the surface used in built-up areas, with transverse furrows which warn you that you're inside an area, in case you haven't noticed the signs in the road.'

"'*In* the road?' said I.

"'Yes,' said he, 'in the road, where the eye rests naturally and where they can't be obscured. Where else would you put them—out at the side?'

"'No,' I said, rather uneasily, 'I don't think I would, but——'

"'Here's an example,' said the driver, and, sure enough, there was a broad band painted across the road surface, red on the left half, and blue on the right. As we passed over it, the sudden change in the sound of our travel showed that the surface had altered.

"'If any one went too fast over this,' said the driver, 'the noise of his tyres would give him away at once—and one of us would have his number before he'd gone very far.'

"'*One of us?*' I said, 'then you're . . .'

"'Oh, yes,' he said, 'I'm in the Road Corps—that's why it was my job to help you. And if I see a case of dangerous driving—which is easy to spot, even if it's impossible to define—in goes the car's

number to headquarters, the same as a case of damage or litter or anything.

"'The point is that no one knows if the man he cuts in front of is Road Corps or not. He may look like a commercial traveller—and he may be one too. His only qualifications are that he's driven 50,000 miles without accident, that he's passed in running repairs and first aid and has a clean record.'

Turner's Reach.

"'But,' said I, 'doesn't this give him too much authority——?'

"'Oh, no,' he said, 'there's no tyranny about it. A report only means a warning notice to the owner. It takes three reports by different officers of the Corps, before any action's taken.'

"'And the penalties?'

"'Three reports means three months off the road —and more if the record's bad.'

"'For the owner?'

"'No—for the car. That makes the owner not only cautious for himself but equally careful of any one else, like chauffeurs and young sons home for the holidays.'

124

"'Well,' I said, 'this is all very new to me. It's a pity it isn't in force everywhere—especially if all these flowers are part of the show.'

"'They are,' he said. 'They really started accidentally, as it were, like so many things in this country. They began, so I've heard, with some fellow's broadcast talk on 'The Open Road.' He remarked what a happy and kindly thought it was to put flowers along the road outside one's garden as well as in it, and asked for cuttings to plant.

"'Well, of course, it turned out that every one with a garden had cuttings, and then local pride came in, and I think it was really these road-garden schemes as much as anything that first made Britain the world's touring ground. For the charm of touring is in the little things near you, just as much as in the scenery in the background.'

"'Well,' I said, 'it all sounds very revolutionary. . . .'

"'Revolutionary?' said he. 'You haven't heard half of it—I haven't told you about this car, and all the others, presented free by the manufacturers because we popularize motoring, instead of scaring people off the roads—and free petrol and upkeep,

and of course no tax, as we're Government servants. I haven't told you how ugly country hoardings were killed by taxes, and ugly country buildings by rates, or how night-driving was revolutionized by the reflector-stud, or how town traffic jams were cured by a special city tax or——'

"'Here,' I said, 'stop—I'm getting quite dizzy. . . .'

"'Quite what?' said he.

"'Quite dizzy,' I said—and sure enough I was. The road suddenly blurred, the noise of the car increased to a roar, and . . .

*   *   *   *   *

"'That's better,' said a strange voice over me.

"I opened my eyes, and looked up at its owner.

"'What's better?' I inquired.

"'You are,' said the voice. 'Run into the van be'ind my engine, you did, wot with getting into a skid and I don't know wot all. Knocked silly you was.'

"Slowly I sat up, and looked sadly round at the old familiar crossroad.

"'I wouldn't call it that,' I said."

" Sorry, but I'm a stranger here."

SECTION XVI

FIGURE STUDIES

" What is he doing, the great God Pan ? "

Famous
Last Words

" As a matter of
fact, I drive better
when I've had a
couple."

(a) *How to estimate average speed*

IF the time taken to travel 100 miles is known, the final column in the following table will give the corrected average speed:

Distance travelled in miles	Time taken in hours	Average speed in miles per hour	
		Neglecting stops	Allowing for stops
100	3	38·3	38·3
,,	4	38·3	38·3
,,	5	38·3	38·3
,,	6	38·3	38·3
,,	7	38·3	38·3
,,	8	38·3	38·3
,,	9	38·3	38·3
,,	10	38·3	38·3

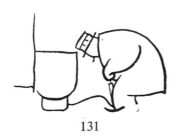

(b) *Composition of Petrol*

Petrol is a compound, composed of C and H, which combines with O to make an explosive mixture, thus:

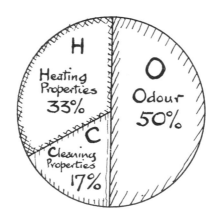

(c) *Lubrication Chart*

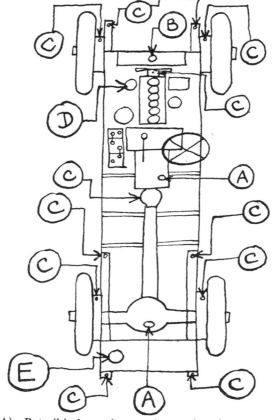

(A) Put oil in here whenever it goes *burr-burr*
(B) Put water in here whenever it goes *buzz-buzz*
(C) Put grease in here whenever it goes *squeak-squeak*
(D) Put oil in here whenever it goes *wump-wump*
(E) Put petrol in here whenever it doesn't go at all

(d) *Effect of various factors on normal running speed*

Wet weather	subtract	5 m.p.h.
Dry weather	add	5 m.p.h.
Car just behind	add	5 m.p.h.
Car hooting just behind	add	10 m.p.h.
30 mile limit sign	subtract	5 m.p.h.
Delimit sign	add	20 m.p.h.
Dangerous corner sign	nil.	
Dangerous hill sign	nil.	
Wreck by roadside	subtract	10 m.p.h.
Recent wreck by roadside	subtract	30 m.p.h.
Dangerous crossroads sign	nil.	
Main well-surfaced road with good visibility	add	10 m.p.h.
Main well-surfaced road with concealed turnings	add	10 m.p.h.
School sign	nil.	
Puddles and/or Pedestrians	nil.	
Police car	subtract £5 or add one month.	

Beauty spot		nil.
Passenger	add	5 m.p.h.
Entertaining passenger	add	10 m.p.h.
Enchanting passenger		stop.

(e) *Average composition of one mile of British road*

Grass and weeds	10 grains
Trees	8 bushels
Tramways	2 trachms
Litter baskets	2 scruples
Barbed wire	9 hanks
Warning notices	1 rood
Telegraphs and telephones	80 poles
Advertisement hoardings	20 decibels

135

Public-houses	4 pints
Tea-rooms	3 pecks
Garages	2 gallons
Banks	5 dwt.
New housing schemes	10 new ohms
Open country	a trace

(f) *Tipping Ready Reckoner*

When breaking your journey at an hotel, a sum equal to 10% of the bill should be distributed among the staff.

This should be divided as follows:

Table waiter or waitress	6% of bill.
Housemaid	3% ,, ,,
Porter who takes luggage up to room	3% ,, ,,
Porter who brings luggage down again next morning (unless it is the same man, which it never is)	3% ,, ,,
Head Porter, who joins his subordinates to wave you good-bye, and who naturally cannot receive less than them	3% ,, ,,
Garage attendant	2% ,, ,,
Garage attendant (the other being after all merely a man standing about in the garage)	2% ,, ,,
Man dressed as head waiter, who spreads the change from your bill on a plate	3% ,, ,,
Add for mistakes in mental arithmetic, through having to calculate under eye of recipients	5% ,, ,,
Total	10% ,, ,,

Note: For the purposes of tipping, only four values need be considered.

(a) the shilling (used for buying back one's hat from cloakrooms)

(b) the half-crown (the normal unit)

(c) the ten-shilling note (usually presented tightly folded, to confuse it with the pound)

(d) the pound note (usually presented open, to distinguish it from the ten-shilling).

" God's in His heaven, all's right with the world."

𝔉amous
𝔏ast 𝔚ords

" She's about due
for   an   overhaul
now."